BONO BOOK

The Biography of Bono

University Press

CONTENTS

INTRODUCTION

The air crackled with anticipation and excitement and could be felt all around Slane Castle. The biggest band of the 1980s, 1990s, and early 2000s was preparing for one of the best performances of their career. Fittingly, the concert is occurring on March 17, better known as St. Patrick's Day, at a castle close to where they played their first live concert in 1981.

A voice begins ringing out in the darkness, and the lights appear on a single man standing on a platform surrounded by fans. He begins the first line of one of the band's most famous songs. Then he stops and strikes a pose with the microphone held high in the air, letting the audience sing with him.

Few bands in the history of Rock and Roll have had the staying power and dedicated fanbase – largely because they have always been phenomenal, putting their audience first. Bono is one of the primary reasons the band has earned its reputation.

He is known for his energized onstage persona and as a nature activist off-stage. His ability to draw emotions from nearly anyone while still making a point – even a critical one – is nearly unrivaled. That doesn't mean he doesn't have detractors, but many other famous musicians have tried and failed to be as poignant in their music, touching people around the world with his message.

Off-stage, some have considered him pretentious, but that comes with how passionate he is about doing more with his large platform. It has also made him popular with his dedicated fanbase – he does more than just entertain. Watching him live in concert has long been exhilarating. Still, his willingness to work with people of many different ideologies has made him such a notable figure who has moved outside of just the entertainment industry.

On that one surreal night in Ireland, Bono reminded the audience why he had become such a beloved Irish figure. His energy was electric, and his willingness to work to delight the crowd was always blatantly obvious. As the song began to warm up, Bono took off running along the runway, keeping close to the crowd as he raced around to the other end. As he reached it, the song reached a familiar refrain about running. Despite having just run the length of it, that familiar voice blasted out over the microphone, a little breathless but giving the performance everything he had. This was the man who continues to be one of the primary sources of inspiration to so many younger and not-so-young musicians. With an extensive list of popular and famous songs, Bono and U2 have earned their place in Rock history. However, Bono himself has made just as much of an impact on people around the world who have never heard any of his iconic music.

CHAPTER 1

Humble Beginnings

O n May 10, 1960, in Dublin, Ireland, Iris Hewson gave birth to Paul David Hewson, her second son. Her husband, Brendan Robert Hewson, also lived in the home, but the couple was of the two religions that had notoriously not gotten along and caused bloodshed on the island: Roman Catholic and Protestant. Iris had been raised as a part of the Church of Ireland, while Bob was Catholic. The two had agreed that they would raise their first child in Iris's faith while the second would be raised Catholic. While his elder brother, Norman, was raised in a Protestant background, Bono spent more time attending church with his mother than mass with his father. Still, he was raised in both religions that had long been pitted against each other, giving him a unique way of looking at the world. He did not develop a particularly strong belief system for either one of the two religions, instead taking to either of the two. This made him unique even at school because he did not fit into any particular group.

One event that shaped the future musician was losing his mother when he was just 14 years old.

CHAPTER 2

U2

The seemingly idyllic early life of the future star gave way to his tragic teenage years when he appeared to be looking for people who could identify with him and his experiences. He found some likely companions after moving to another school, where he met a group of teens who significantly contributed to his outlook on life. The group referred to themselves as Lypton Village and had a habit of giving each other nicknames. There were various nicknames given to Paul David Hewson, and a number of different meanings have been given to the way each of those nicknames was derived. Over time his nickname was altered and shortened from several longer variations into Bono Vox. It has been said that the name derived from the brand name Bonavox, which is a manufacturer and seller of hearing aids. Initially, the 16-year-old did not like his nickname, but when he was told it meant "good voice," the future star accepted the name. Eventually, his friends just called him Bono, and it is the name that would identify him around the world just a few years later. While 1974 was one of the hardest of his life, 1976 proved to be one that helped Bono to find some stability and a place where he belonged.

During 1976 and 1977, he also started a band with some of his friends from Lypton Village. Bono quickly became the driving force as he took on multiple roles in the band in the early days. He had already learned how to play guitar, wrote the band's songs, and was the lead vocalist. The other band members were David Evans, better known as The Edge, Larry Mullen Jr, and Adam Clayton, who had also become his friend by 1976. All of them were passionate about their music, and each had responded to an advertisement posted to the Mount Temple bulletin board asking for other students who wanted to join together to form a band. This was when they met and became friends. Larry had been the original poster of that message.

However, some problems arose when the band was still fairly new. Though he had taken on the most responsibility, Bono became less critical of the band as David Evans, aka The Edge, became a better guitarist. The band began to rely on The Edge for the music, leaving Bono to handle the vocals. Then the band began to say that his voice just wasn't quite what they wanted going forward, and for a while, they considered kicking him out of the band U2. His approach was different than that of most of the rest of the band. Bono later recounted how losing his mother had helped to launch him into music as a way of coping with her death: "I realized aged 14, when my mother suddenly passed away at her own father's graveside, that I had a hole in my heart... I didn't know at the time, as I filled it with music. I became an artist through her absence, and I owe her for that. I thought the rage I had was a part of rock'n'roll, but the rage was grief." Ultimately, he remained a part of the band, and they decided to keep going after they had all graduated from school.

Even though the band was young, they likely realized that Bono was easily the most charismatic person in the group to act as the frontman. He has always had a stage presence that captures the attention of audiences. Because he has so much enthusiasm and boundless energy, it was clear to the band that Bono would help keep people engaged, especially in the early days. He was also clearly different from many other people in the area as he was willing to engage in new music, particularly the Punk movement. This may have been why the band had considered removing him from the band. Still, he had such amazing energy that they quickly became popular in the area, even if some of his interest was in a musical genre that wasn't very popular. As he stood in front of the audience, it was clear they were connecting with him, and he could interact with them in a way that none of the other band members could. This has become one of the defining parts of U2, and without Bono, it is uncertain just how long the band would have lasted, even if they had been able to make only a handful of their popular songs. Later, people kept coming to their concerts for the charismatic singer because he made them feel like they were part of the show.

Another part of what bonded the band members was that they were all deeply Christian. This has been a part of the defining aspects of the band well into their career, and it proved to be a problem that they had to overcome early as several members considered becoming members at a Christian fellowship. Three of the band members seriously considered making a move. While they didn't join the fellowship, they added many instrumental ideologies to their music. Many of their most popular songs are based on Christian teachings, particularly a drive for peace. It is also a large part of why the band had joined in so many charitable efforts, making political speech a part of who the band was long before they were internationally famous.

Like most bands, U2 started as a cover band, with much of their music focusing on playing their versions of songs by the Beach Boys and Rolling Stones. Bono did begin writing lyrics during this time, and the band started writing their own music. With his interest in the growing Punk genre,

Bono's lyrics helped establish these deeply religious band members as more rebellious instead of simply following what other bands were doing. It was a unique mix that kept attracting people back to watch them. The more they played their own music, the more the audience connected to the music. The music was different, showing a desire for change without calling for chaos or extreme rebellion. It was in stark contrast to most of the other early Punk bands. As people continued to come to see them perform, U2's reputation spread far beyond the local population.

CHAPTER 3

Potential

In May 1979, the band played in Dublin to a raucous crowd near Gaiety Greenmarket. What helped to make a difference was that other younger teenagers could come and enjoy the show. This meant they had a huge audience when one of the scouts, Chas De Whalley from CBS London, arrived. He had been contacted by the band's manager, Paul McGuinness, about the band. He wasn't particularly impressed by the music, but even he said just how captivating Bono was on stage. Bono was mobile and lively, making sure the people were amped up by the band, even if they weren't particularly impressed by the sound the band was making. Though U2 hadn't impressed him, he saw potential in the band, so he returned to London and talked about getting the band to do a demo for CBS London after returning to Ireland.

After watching their performance, he had them join him in a studio to record the demos that CBA London agreed to have done. They were in the studio for six hours and another six hours the next night. At the end of their time in the studio, the band had three tracks called *U2: Three*, and there was a lot of friction around the band then. De Whalley wasn't happy with how their drummer, Larry, was keeping time, saying he wasn't good. He and Larry clashed over the recordings while Bono stood by, angry at how the recording manager handled one of the band members. At the same time, de Whalley was incredibly impressed by how adept The Edge was with a guitar, especially because he wasn't doing what everyone else did. While most musicians played full chords, The Edge broke the chords up and played on open strings. It was a very different style that helped differentiate the band from most other bands playing at that time. Their other guitarist, Adam Clayton, wasn't quite as adept and had a slightly different sense of rhythm than the rest of the band. De Whalley later said that the initial track was a mess, but they managed to make it almost work. Later, this difference among the members helped to differentiate them from everyone else. Instead of being seen as chaotic and messy, their sound became distinctive. The band has become renowned and acclaimed for never making two albums that sounded the same. Every new record is unique and a large part of their staying power. Each band member has their own sense of the music they are playing, and while there is some work to iron out the differences, it leaves much of it up to each member to add their own bit of personality to the music. This has helped to keep them sounding fresh and different for decades.

What worked for them later wasn't a winner in the beginning, though. It took time for them to learn how to make something of the unique sounds, and that first track was not going to win anyone over in London. The band took the tracks and polled their fans, mixing up the music and sounds to see which one the fans thought should be the A side of the three tracks.

De Whalley wasn't the only person who went back to Ireland to check out U2 at home, where bands can act and sound differently. One of the men who watched them after they returned was named Tom Nolan, who worked for EMI and watched them in July. Like De Walley, he was impressed by their live sound, going back to watch them the next day when they played at Gaiety Green. He later recalled what he thought of the band, particularly Bono; "The audience were quite young, 13 to 18, and Bono was so confident. He fell off-stage and lowered himself into the crowd like a real big-time rock star. It was a real group with four people in it, all doing a specific job, like the Beatles or the early Stones. But it wasn't rock music, and it certainly wasn't punk, it was something else. Kind of atonal. It was strange and eerie, with a lot of echo from Edge's guitar." The primary difference between Nolan and De Whalley was that Nolan had some Irish heritage, so when he listened to the music, he said that there was a sense of something Celtic behind their music. He pointed to the way Bono behaved as being very Irish, even saying, "Bono's definitely got that Irish literary thing, I saw that straight away...I thought he was very artistic in an Irish kind of way – he had an interest in genuine art. I don't think he saw himself as a rock star." This Irishness came across as the band started to get bigger, and Bono talked to the crowd with his Irish accent

That same summer, Dave McCullough, a writer for the Northern Irish Sounds, convinced the paper's editor that they should do a full spread on an Irish band that he loved – of course, the band was U2. When he met with the band, Bono stood out because he was very opinionated and not afraid to voice those opinions. They went to Ringsend Power Station, where the band was photographed for the spread, and those images helped inspire one of their later album covers. Unfortunately, only one roll of film was taken of them as the photographer was eager to leave, saying it was really cold for August. Nevertheless, the spread helped to gain them more attention, leading to one of the songs from their track being released, "Out of Control." It quickly went to the top of the charts in Ireland. The band had 1,000 copies of the record, and it sold out the day it went up for sale.

With U2 getting more traction and coverage in Ireland, De Whalley was able to return, hoping to get something better from this trip. This time, he didn't go alone. Someone else joined him from his company, but a few men from the rival company A&R showed up to check out the band, seemingly taking Ireland by storm. Although the band didn't perform anything spectacular that night, the record companies' scouts went to see them, and their manager was a strong advocate, as always. He ensured that everyone who had come to scout the band from London was up at the front to get a full feel for the energy the band brought. By the end of the concert, De Whallcy said, "It wasn't a fantastic gig but it was OK, ...I think Muff was ready to offer them a deal on the strength of my enthusiasm and the momentum growing in Ireland. This would have put them on a roster including The Clash and The Only Ones." Had they been signed, U2 would have ended up on the same label as two big American musicians, Bob Dylan and Bruce Springsteen. However, the deal did not go through.

Their attempts to break out onto a larger platform failed as long as they remained in Ireland, and the band quickly reached a breaking point. Their time to find success as musicians would end soon because The Edge had made a deal with his parents that if he didn't succeed as a musician, he would go to school to become an engineer. In the hopes of finally making it, the band planned to go to the UK to see if their energy and sound could translate there.

CHAPTER 4

Success

When U2 struck out to become successful musicians, they were in one of the worst places in Europe to get started in the music industry. Ireland was still considered a backwater place for music. The band's timing and punk-influenced sound came at nearly a perfect time, though, because Ireland finally launched a pop radio station. There was a need for the station to find bands who could contribute music to their programming. They focused on finding local people instead of looking at the UK and US for bands. The idea was to push for local musicians to create heroes who could speak to the Irish audience. Bands and musicians often discussed political matters, but those concerns weren't typically relevant to the Irish, who had their own problems to overcome. U2 seemed to bridge the religious divide in the nation because they were of mixed Christian religions, which was big in the country at the time. As teenagers, they had an energy that drew people into their music, and with a frontman who could connect with the audience in concerts, they quickly became a favorite band across the country. Bill Graham (an Irish journalist and author) was one of their earliest champions, comparing their type of punk to the type in the UK by saying, "If British punk screamed 'No Future,' Irish youth had more reason to shout 'No Past.'" Instead of championing chaos and a sense that the future was bleak, U2's music was more hopeful and championed working together and improving the situation. Their message gave a sense of hope in a movement that felt untethered.

That doesn't mean that it was easy. Initially, the band went through the same problems most bands experience. Those who attended their earliest concerts said the group was rubbish and hadn't yet found their sound or message. Then one of their guitarists, Dick Evans, left the band, though his brother Dave remained as one of the founding members. They even went through several names, including Feedback and The Hype, before finally settling on U2. After that, their sound shifted into a much more obvious punk tone. By early 1978, they were good enough to win a St Patrick's Day talent contest in the Irish city of Limerick. This earned them 500 pounds and an amazing opportunity to record their music for CBS Ireland. Soon after, Paul

McGuinness joined them as their manager. The band gave him a name as well, calling him The Goose.

The band was different from many other early bands because they were against the idea of the kind of hedonistic lifestyle that most musicians maintained, especially when they were on tour. More interested in maintaining a connection with their faith, the band members seemed to keep themselves grounded by taking a different approach as they became more popular around Ireland and soon around the UK. When they left Ireland, they were among the biggest local bands in Dublin. Bono had also been taking lessons with Irish actors Conal Kearney and Mannix Flynn, learning to hold the audience's attention. As a result, his presence on stage appeared to be entirely easy and natural, but he also made sure that he knew some of the tricks that actors used, and he was incredibly effective at keeping his concerts lively.

Their initial start in the UK was not particularly brilliant. When they decided to tour outside of Ireland in 1979, the four-member band looked more closely aligned with the Punk genre, with their style most closely aligned with *The Clash* and *The Sex Pistols*, than the wider Rock genre. In December 1979, they were touring around Great Britain, attracting very small crowds – they were still teenagers at the time. They had been billed as V2 instead of U2, showing just how little known they were. Still, they kept going, hoping that they would ultimately attract the attention of someone who would be interested in signing them to a contract. They were aware of just how lucky they were to be able to tour at all, as their funding had fallen through not long before they were scheduled to leave on their tour. When family and friends helped fund their trip, the teens were able to head out in the hopes that they would be able to start a serious career in music. Also, just before their departure, The Edge had been in an accident, and though the car accident was minor, he had to bandage his hand for a good bit of the tour. In significant pain during one of their concerts, he lost his temper when one of the strings on his guitar snapped. He stormed off of the set - in front of talent scouts. This upset was followed by a serious argument with a sound man who assisted the band when they talked about religion, which happened again over the years. At the end of their short tour, in which they didn't reach nearly as many people as they did back home, the band tried to record a single for one of the studios. Still, it was said to be the nail in the band's coffin as Bono's voice was adversely affected by the series of concerts they had just given. All of the promises they had found in Ireland seemed to have amounted to nothing once they tried to expand outside their own country. Their time traveling yielded nothing except some bad memories of the UK.

Their lives changed when they returned to Ireland,

as The Edge had told his parents he would earn an engineering degree if their music career did not take off during their time traveling in 1979. Unfortunately, all the labels they tried to join had turned them down.

As it appeared, they were ready to break up, and other less well-known labels were interested in getting the band to sign contracts with them. However, the series of unfortunate events captured the attention of some of the people who had seen them, including some journalists. What had seemed like a failed trip had gained the group a considerable amount of attention in the UK for the same reason that people back in Ireland had taken an interest in them. Bono drew them in when playing live, and the music had its own interesting quality that no other band had at that time. The lyrics were a part of the attraction, as they were passionate about what they were doing.

They also had a very tenacious manager in Paul McGuinness. Though he had failed to secure the money to help them travel, he was very diligent in helping to get people to pay attention to the band. As long as he could get the band up in front of a crowd, Bono's energy tended to do the rest. They may not have had much chance of signing with one of the big labels in their early days, but very few bands managed that in their first round. And it seemed to help them as U2 was able to negotiate a much better deal with a smaller label. The fact that they ended up being able to take control of so much more is likely the thing that helped them to become the powerhouse they became. Many bands sign contracts under terms that favor the label, making it difficult for the band to thrive. Thanks partly to McGuinness, they avoided one of the worst pitfalls of the music industry.

CHAPTER 5

America

The band had a rough time getting the attention they needed to make a career with their music, but overall, in 1979, McGuinness was very active in making sure that people heard about the band and took the time to check them out. His tireless work and shrewd moves helped to get the band the kind of attention and buzz that most bands never have. However, Bono's stage presence often charmed people into taking the band more seriously.

After a less-than-stellar performance in the UK, most of the enthusiasm that had been building in record companies outside of Ireland was dwindling. It was the indie scene that swooped in and changed the future of the band. One of the biggest indie labels was Chris Blackwell's Island Records, who had also signed Bob Marley much earlier. McGuinness had been trying to get their attention, but the label had only a few UK bands when the 80s began. Getting in touch with Rob Partridge, one of the Island's member's press office, McGuinness sent over some demo tapes for Partridge and publicist Neil Storey to listen to. It was The Edge who attracted their attention because his sounds were so haunting and unique. However, getting more interest in the group took some work, resulting in more scouts being sent to watch the band live. It was Bono who they walked away remembering. Bono had done one of his impromptu sermons at a show they attended in Belfast, which resulted in someone heckling him about shutting up and playing. One of the people who attended remembered that Bono did not react in the way that many other musicians did; "He probably just totally ignored it, or joined in. He always had a cockiness, a cheekiness that was really appealing. I don't think he's ever really been a sex symbol, but there is just a presence, a magnetism. He has the ability to draw you into their music." This remained true long after the band found itself going up in the charts.

With the people who saw the band reporting back how fresh and vibrant the band was, one of the higher-ups at Island Records finally started listening. Nick Bill Stewart ended up listening to the band's demos while on a cricket tour around East Africa. He found that he enjoyed the music and played it so that some of the others with him could listen too. Most of the people who listened enjoyed the music. When he returned to London, one of the first things he did was to contact McGuinness, who invited Stewart to watch the band at the National Boxing Stadium in Dublin. It was an incredibly wise move by McGuinness. By playing a large venue, it changed the sound, as well as allowed for a much larger audience. Since U2 was still adored around Ireland, there was a large turnout to watch the band, which was exactly what Stewart saw. He later recounted what he witnessed that day, saying, "The band came on and played '11 O'Clock Tick Tock Tock' and the stage was invaded. After about four numbers, I turned to Michael Deeny, who's the godfather of Irish music, and said, 'For fuck's sake! This is the Led Zeppelin of the 1980s!" I knew I was watching something special. Musically, I found them a little naive, but the way they got their own crowd going, the way Bono handled it.... I just thought, 'I've got to have this band.'"

He still had to convince Blackwell that the band needed to be signed to a contract, which wasn't easy to do. Stewart had just lost one band that he had been eager to sign, a band that had a lot of parallels with U2 – one of the other big bands of the 1980s and 1990s, REM. Several people pushed him to sign the young band, and a contract was drafted. The deal ended up being much more long-term than most other deals, though it was not a particularly large deal. In many ways, it was U2's last chance after being turned down by so many other labels. It turned out to be the best deal that the band could get. They were still very rough around the edges – why so many labels had rejected them – but that was perfect for the indie label. It was a mutually beneficial arrangement because the label was investing in U2, giving them a chance to grow into their music while the band had the funding to keep going. What was initially known as Nick Stewart's Folly proved to be a complete failure by the other record labels to follow the advice of those who had experienced the band live. On recordings, people were drawn to The Edge's unique music. In person, it was Bono who kept people interested and engaged. Everyone who saw the band in those early days repeated this sentiment over and over, and it has remained true over most of the band's albums.

Steps were finally made to help the band learn to make a more polished sound, but it was not meant to stifle the band the way most labels did. Instead, it was to help them learn to work with the four unique components of the band. After some hard work, they finally started their first full album, *Boy*. During this time, the band struck those who worked with them as being very different from the other up-and-coming bands. Compared to the downer-intellectual music most bands of the time played, U2 was lively and positive. While other bands seemed measured and calculated, U2 was rare and alive. Perhaps the label liked the most was that the band members were serious and focused. They weren't interested in just money and cars – they wanted to be successful as musicians. Their religious perspective was not inclined to the hedonism that plagued many other bands as they found success. Even though they were still young, U2 was mature regarding their approach to their music, and they weren't going to waste time on things that didn't matter.

They were easily one of the fastest bands to learn how to handle their rising name. Reported to be media savvy, the band learned early that they needed to have quotes that would make the headlines. That job was left up to Bono, who quickly saw that the people who reported on the musicians weren't interested in the music but in the stories, the band could tell. When it came to telling stories and being memorable, Bono has always been among the best in music.

Still, the band didn't seem to speak to people in the UK. Their first album only had 8,000 copies and did not sell particularly well. Ireland still loved the band, but it wasn't going to be able to sustain U2's musical career. Since the UK couldn't appreciate them, U2 decided to look for an audience across the Atlantic. In December 1980, they played in New York City. Their stay in the states was extended to 3 months in what was the biggest music market around the globe. It was a definite gamble, but it paid off as American audiences were far more receptive to the young band, especially as the young

Irishmen were willing to play small venues all over the country, not just in a few key cities. By reaching out to a much wider audience, U2 accomplished what few other British bands accomplished – finding success in the US.

CHAPTER 6

Fame

U2 was growing in popularity, having broken through the American music market. Their religious beliefs, which could be found in their music, resonated with Americans across the Bible Belt and the Midwest. Their unique sound and lively performances won over most of the rest of the country, with the band becoming popular at the same time as REM, an American band that also had a very unique sound and different take on music. Both bands spoke to the discontentment felt by younger generations while still sounding largely upbeat. Both bands also had some very interesting singers who contributed to the band's image. However, there were a lot of differences between the two bands, particularly the singers. There wasn't any other frontman like Bono.

The band began touring in support of their third

album in 1982, and soon they proved that they had the ability to be as big as some people had predicted earlier. They rounded out their tour back home, playing for three nights for the fans who had supported them long before anyone else even recognized them. They played their last song of the tour on Christmas Eve, and it was a song that spoke to their audience. It is one of the most well-known songs the band has written, and it appeared on what is usually considered their breakout album, which is their third album, *War*. As the name indicates, they were far more open and outspoken about their world views and politics. They released a single on January 1, 1983, called "New Year's Day." During a time of political turmoil, the record resonated with people at the time. However, Bono's impressive vocals and the way The Edge played the piano on the song caught people's attention. The single shot up on the charts with a far more polished sound and a relatable ideology. It became a frequently played song on the new MTV and radio stations across the US. Europe, particularly the UK, finally started playing U2's music, which was just as big a hit across the continent. It was the first time one of their songs reached the Top 10 singles in the UK. The video included images of war interspersed with images of the band standing in the snow. Bono's presence is obvious, even in this video, as he has a presence that makes the viewer feel like he is singing to them. Today, the song is still played on radios across the world. At the time, the single prepared the world for a new kind of album.

When *War* was released, it went gold, then platinum as the band became famous across the western world. It also gave the band their first Number 1 album in the UK (a feat they have done nine more times by 2022). However, perhaps the most impressive accomplishment of their breakout album was the fact that when it reached the Number 1 spot in the UK, it replaced Michael Jackson's *Thriller*.

While the album was mixed, it included some of the band's most iconic songs, including the last song of their tour the previous year, "Sunday Bloody Sunday." It was a song filled with political meaning for Ireland, demonstrating the willingness of the band to speak up about politically charged themes from very early in their career. Since they probably remembered the events of that day on a more personal level, it helped remind the world where the young men came from while showing their desire for reconciliation.

Their fourth album, *The Unforgettable Fire*, proved that they were able to keep writing music that people could easily love. Perhaps the best-known song is "Pride," which is often called "In the Name of Love." Another incredibly popular song from the album is "Bad."

The band had established themselves in the music industry, and they were frequently sought out for live shows, particularly Bono, who by this point had shown what had attracted people to the band in their early days. Given how interested the band was in political causes, someone from Amnesty International approached them about joining their tour called "Conspiracy of Hope," which was meant to make people aware of the human rights violations occurring worldwide and to start fighting against it. Bono quickly signed up, joining the international organization as they went around South America. He saw the effects of war in Nicaragua and El Salvador. He became a philanthropist after seeing how violence and poverty had harmed the majority of people in those countries.

With the experience fresh on Bono's mind, the band joined Live Aid, which was a concert held in two places – London and Philadelphia, in July 1985. TV stations arrived to record the event that was raising awareness of Ethiopia's famine and raising money to help them. It is estimated that about 1.5 billion people tuned in to see many popular bands playing their most popular songs. With four albums under their belt, the last two albums proving to have a lot of very popular songs, and a lively frontman, U2 was one of the most eagerly awaited bands set to play. Other big bands played included Crosby, Stills, Nash, Young, The Who, and Black Sabbath. Having lost their drummer in an accident, Led Zeppelin was set to join the concert, with the rising drummer Phil Collins playing drums during their time on stage. Collins appeared both in London and in Philadelphia. He had played with his band Genesis in London early in the day, then crossed the Atlantic to join Led Zeppelin in the US.

As big as these bands were, a large percentage of people who tuned in to watch the London bands were tuning in to see the famous band, Queen, whose famously boisterous and impressive singer, Freddy Mercury, and the little band out of Ireland, U2. With the two concert venues switching between each other, U2 was set to play in London after Bryan Adams finished his time in Philadelphia and while the Beach Boys set up to play after him. The actor Jack Nicholson introduced the band, saying they were "a group that's never had any problem saying how they feel," U2 took the stage, ready to start with one of their best songs, "Sunday Bloody Sunday." What is impressive is that the singer's voice was just as powerful and moving in his live performance as it was on the recording. During their first song, he was far more muted in terms of his interactions with the crowd than he typically was. He even seemed slightly uncomfortable with how limited he was up on stage. Toward the middle of the song, he moved down into the space between the stage and the audience, calling for them to sing with him, saying, "You know the words!" As the song neared its conclusion, he returned to the stage to rejoin his bandmates. The song ended with raucous applause, and people continued to sing the catchy chorus.

They were set to play two more songs, including "Pride," but U2 ended up going off script for their second song, "Bad." Bono had a habit of ensuring that the audience was always engaged and felt a part of the music, kissing people in the crowd, climbing on the equipment, and climbing up to the balcony during a concert at the Boston Orpheum Theatre. He was not accustomed to being constricted to a stage, which had gotten to the energetic performer. With a full stadium, he managed to get through nearly half of the song before doing what he did best, entertaining his audience. It was obvious he was getting antsy by adlibbing new lyrics and dancing around with the guitarists. At one point, he dropped the mic and headed to the ramp he had taken during the first song. He waved at the audience, trying to get them to sing the song back to him now that there was no mic, and many of the fans were reaching back toward him. When one woman overcame a barrier, he decided to break away on his own, jumping off the stage and waving for others to join him. When a woman was pulled out of the audience to join him, she hugged him, and the famous lead singer began to dance with her, holding her tight. He was then taken back to a ladder so that he could make his way back up onstage, where a few more women waited.

He later stated, "I'd gone AWOL to try and find a television moment and forgot about the song." Since he often pulled people onto the stage to join him, he decided he needed to take the stage to the audience. Once back on stage, he sang pieces of several other songs while their time wound down.

The concert was 16 hours long and included some of the biggest names of the 1980s. However, of all the many performances, none made the impact that U2 did, largely because of how dedicated Bono was to making the most of interaction with the audience, not just for them. Performances by Queen that day were iconic, but what most people of the time remembered for long after that day was how U2 proved why they were a band who cared not just about music but about people. The Edge later described the moment, "Looking back, as I did a week later, I started to see what it was. It was the sense of real, total jeopardy, which is always very exciting for a live event. Bono's complete determination to make physical contact with the crowd and eventually get there after two minutes of struggling over barriers. I think there was something about the effort he had to put in to do it that somehow made it even more powerful." The events of that day are still available and easy to find online, making this iconic part of rock history something that can still be seen today, and The Edge was quite right in his assessment. Bono's desire to interact was captivating in all the right ways. He also received criticism because it wasn't what had been planned, and there was an element of uncertainty to it. But for him, it also seemed more than worth the risk to make sure people were having a good time.

CHAPTER 7

Joshua Tree

U2 had gone from being a largely beloved band in Ireland to a beloved Irish band across the world by 1987. Their very different performance at Live Aid in 1985 resulted in their records selling incredibly well in the years immediately following the event. But their next album made them the legendary band that remained on the charts for decades.

Inspired by what he had seen when traveling with Amnesty International, Bono had a different take on the music, which showed in U2's music. The idea for the name of the next album was originally *The Two Americas*, and they wanted to show the different perspectives of one of the most powerful nations in the world. It was a picture that showed two very different sides, and as foreigners, the band members felt like outsiders. They were looking at the nation that had helped them break out and make their musical career a reality, but they were taking a more critical look, as they did with everything. They were looking at the stark differences between the massive country in the album and the idea of the desert colliding with civilization ended up making the cover. They traveled to some of the hottest parts of North America, including Death Valley, the Mojave Desert, Zabriskie Point, and the abandoned town called Bodie. It was when the photographer Anton Corbijn decided to show Bono one of his favorite trees found in the American deserts. Bono brought a *Bible* with him to look at the tree and found the tree named in the *Bible*, not only finding the cover for their album but the title for it as well. That's how one of the best albums in music history was named *The Joshua Tree*.

Nor was the image easy to capture. Considering they were in the desert in the middle of December, it was incredibly cold. They decided to take off their coats to point out that they were in a desert. They lasted about 20 minutes getting pictures of the band in front of the solo tree without coats. Bono later explained that being out in the freezing conditions caused them to look so dour. However, their look on the cover hinted at the more serious songs on the record. Unfortunately, the tree captured on the album died in 2000, meaning it can no longer be visited.

Bono later said that 1986 was a rough year for him,

and he spent most of the year on the road touring and getting ideas for the next song. His wife was upset by the amount of time he was gone, and as an apology to her, he wrote a song that was originally going to be put on this iconic album, but no one in the band felt that it was ready to be released. "Sweetest Thing" was polished and released as a single. He tried to get the song to her by her birthday but failed. This gave him and the band time to clean up the tracks, and when they finally released it, the song was incredibly well-received. It was a departure from their early works, both because it was a love song and because it was far more in the Pop genre than any of the other songs. It was released as a single because Bono's wife insisted that all the money the song earned go to Children of Chernobyl.

Most of the rest of the record includes music inspired by several American genres that were less popular or well-known: Blues, Gospel, and Folk. The songs on the album were a new sound for the band and incredibly well-received by their fans. Having been hyped up for what the band would do next during Live Aid, fans were ready to buy whatever U2 published. They were treated to some of the most well-known songs the band has ever written, including "I Still Haven't Found What I'm Looking For," "Where the Streets Have No Name," and "With or Without You."

During 1987, the band seemed to either want to

distance themselves from the big name their band had earned or desired the kind of connection with the audience that they had in concerts in their early days. As a result, they created a second band, named "Dalton Brothers," suggesting the four members were all brothers. A few times, Dalton Brothers opened for U2, playing country music before the popular Irish band started to play. It was a departure from their usual music, but the band played their country songs and covered a few other artists. With gallon hats and massive wigs, only those up close could see that the four men on stage weren't a country band, but U2 playing country music before playing all of the songs that people had come to love by the band.

The Joshua Tree remains the band's best-selling album, with over 25 million albums sold to date (making it also one of the best-selling records in history). In addition, it is considered to have cultural significance in the US and is preserved in the US Library of Congress. As if to hint at just how successful the record would be, over 1 million tickets were sold within the first 24 hours when the tour tickets went on sale. Given the lasting popularity of so many songs on the record, it is still considered one of the best-recorded records. This trend toward more popular musical genres would continue, with *All That You Can't Leave Behind*, released in 2000, sounding more like their first few albums, with the maturity and polish they had gained over the two decades in the spotlight.

CHAPTER 8

Astonishing Career

U2 has always been a difficult band to put into any one genre because they take inspiration from nearly every available genre. This is perhaps most readily obvious when comparing The Joshua Tree and Achtung Baby, released in 1991. One is soulful, taking a lot of its tone and political criticism from more somber genres. The other has a much greater influence by pop and other genres. They spent much of the 1990s trying out new styles. Pop was perhaps the worst received because it was experimental in a way that didn't connect.

Bono would later say of one of their most critically acclaimed albums, *How to Dismantle an Atomic Bomb*, "It's the best collection of songs we've put together. But as an album, the whole isn't greater than the sum of its parts, and it fucking annoys me." This reflects how Bono was far more critical of his works than people's, focusing on quality over anything else. Knowing that the songs were more like what people had loved (after a few less popular releases), he wanted people to have access.

Critics and fans agreed with his assessment, at least in part. The album won nine Grammy nominations between 2005 and 2006, including the coveted Album of the Year. Some have said that this was more a way of recognizing the band for their phenomenal contribution to music than a recognition of the music on the album. During this time, U2 was inducted into the Rock and Roll Hall of Fame, which points to the awards trying to make up for not recognizing the band when they really should have been recognized. It seemed more like a way of playing catchup or correcting themselves. When playing live, U2 generally only played two of the songs that appeared on the album.

As cell phones became more common, the band agreed to something that would have been incredibly popular a decade earlier – they released their 2014 album for free on all iPhones. The problem was that the times had shifted, and most people purchasing the phones were of a generation that had no real knowledge of the band and how it interacted with its fans. *Songs of Innocence* was free for everyone who had iTunes, but this proved to be more of an annoyance than something people wanted. Some felt it was proof that the band was out of touch with what people wanted, thinking that they were so beloved that everyone would want their latest song. Others were annoyed that their limited space was being taken up by a band they didn't know and weren't willing to give them a chance. They missed the fact that U2 has always tried to please their fans, and given the band's outspoke perspectives, particularly Bono's, they were trying to do something that would ensure that anyone who wanted their music could get it. In retrospect, a better approach would have been to let people know that the album was free to download instead of simply adding it without confirmation that people wanted it, but the technology was still so new at the time. Trying to let people know that it was free probably wouldn't have reached a majority of people. Expecting people to figure out how to download it was also problematic, as older generations were less likely to take the time to learn. It seemed like the path of least resistance to make sure that people had a pleasant surprise. Instead, it attracted more negative publicity. Given how people had been looking for a way to download songs for free since Napster was shut down, U2 was letting their fans know that they were clearly on the side of free music.

Unfortunately, the record became known for this controversy because the songs were more of a return to form for the band. It had music inspired by the genres that had made the band so popular.

Whatever people may feel about the band, their legacy is long and has proven to be lasting, as much of their music is still played today. Many of their songs are viewed as anthems for their times, but they still have relevance today. Because they didn't stick to a single genre, it is nearly impossible to detect in which decades most of the songs were written. Many of them could have been popular had they been released today as they were in 1983 or 1991.

CHAPTER 9

Charitable Causes

T hough he wasn't the only lyricist in the band, Bono was the primary writer, which has clarified his stance on many different areas. From his early days developing as a rock star, he was an enthusiastic social activist. His performance at Live Aid was just one of many charitable causes. He clearly married someone who was just as conscious of the world, considering she had a personal song written for her turned into a hit that would benefit her favorite charity.

Following the devastation of Hurricane Katrina, U2 joined another popular band from the 1990s and early 2000s, Green Day. Together, the two iconic bands covered "The Saints Are Coming" to earn money for the survivors and help rebuild the famous and unique city of New Orleans. There was nothing in it for the bands considering none of the members came from the state, let alone the area. It was an effort to help where they could, especially as the world watched in horror at the federal government's slow response after the flooding began. Just one year later, the band recorded a song on *Instant Karma; The Amnesty International Campaign to Save Darfur*. They were one of many popular bands to contribute and were one of the reasons so many people were interested in buying the track (as well as to benefit Darfur).

Bono has long been an outspoken musician, which led to him transitioning into trying to work with world leaders, many of whom had grown up loving his music. For several decades, he has divided his time between music and politics, which is partly why they have seen longer periods between records. He was one of the founders of Debt, AIDS, Trade, Africa, better known as DATA, to help people across the continent with various problems, particularly poverty, hunger, and AIDS. He wasn't afraid to work with people that did not align with his beliefs, most notably former US President George W. Bush. People were angry with him for working with a president who was polarizing and helped embroil the US in two wars during his presidency. The critics of the move failed to understand that Bono was more interested in accomplishing goals than shunning unpopular figures. The US was in the country in the best place to help fight AIDS, so Bono was willing to work with the president, regardless of their stance and criticism against them. When he traveled with the US Treasury Secretary across Africa, people began to see the work as a way for conservatives and liberals to learn to work together to help fight problems, starting with poverty.

Bono was also one of the co-founders of the ONE Campaign in 2004, just two years after he traveled to Africa with a US representative. He then went on to help start Red, a part of the ONE Campaign to help fight the spread of AIDS in Africa. By 2010, he started largely keeping his activism out of the public eye.

The man is a curious example of just how much people can do and achieve. Queen Elizabeth II knighted the Irish man in 2007. He has proven to be an adept businessman, cofounding Elevation Partners, an investment capital business. Like much of what he's done, Bono has been criticized for this business. Some saying that he is managing to not fully pay his taxes because of the business, to which he has pushed back, saying that being a philanthropist doesn't mean he should be a pushover in business. This is in line with the cheeky comments he would give hecklers when they told him to stop with the sermons and start singing.

He has had a couple of health scares over the years, with the first occurring in the spring of 2010 while rehearsing for a concert in Germany. His emergency surgery was successful, but it meant cutting back their tour. When he fully recovered, he made sure to make up all the canceled shows. Then, he was in a serious bike accident in 2014 while in New Yorke City. Recovery was much harder as he suffered numerous serious injuries, and it wasn't clear if he would be able to play guitar again. He has called it both a "Major brush with mortality" and an "extinction event" that made him stop and consider his life. More recently, he was hospitalized with a possible throat cancer diagnosis. Fortunately, he didn't have the disease, meaning the disease or any treatment would not destroy his famous vocals. Even his famous glasses, which have been a part of his image for decades, were not exactly a choice. In 2014, he and U2 were on *The Graham Norton Show* when he finally talked about his glasses: "This is a good place to explain to people that I've had glaucoma for the last 20 years. I have good treatments and I am going to be fine." What some people have thought was pretentious resulted from a health condition that he didn't want to discuss. Bono hasn't been that big about talking about himself, choosing to keep the conversation on music or the causes he cares about. However, that doesn't mean that he won't talk about them, as it became clear when it was announced that the legendary singer is releasing a book of memoirs of highs and lows that most people will never experience. Titled *Surrender: 40 Songs, One Story*, the book recounts Bono's life, and each chapter is named after a U2 song, giving it a unique take that only a musician with such a unique legacy could accomplish.

CONCLUSION

I t is difficult to say whether Bono made his name because of his music or activism. Those who grew up listening to U2 would unequivocally say that his music brought him to the world stage and made him memorable. Younger generations tend to have much less knowledge of the band, with many not even realizing what songs the band has written or how significant their impact has been on the musical industry. To these generations, Bono is more of a curiosity which seems to preach more than play. They fail to understand that U2, particularly Bono, has long embodied the kind of musical political activism that helped to create other musical legends, like Bob Dylan, John Lennon, and Bob Marley. Growing up in Ireland in the 1960s and 1970s, they were surrounded by politics, sometimes a life or death situation. Their brand always had politics baked into the foundations, and it was a matter of doing more as they achieved more. Bono has never shied away from speaking out about what he feels is right – not because he has a platform now, but because he always felt it was important. Nor does he insist that people agree with him because what he has always wanted was to help bring people together. It is part of what has made him so beloved by those who grew up listening to his lyrics and feeling that there was someone who saw that things could be bad but chose to be positive in the hope of making things better. It is a type of boundless optimism that has always rubbed some people the wrong way, but it has also made him and much of the band's outlook and music so memorable.

Made in the USA
Thornton, CO
11/06/22 10:59:38

e3f48b2a-ddaf-4d21-8ff8-39b8f377d264R01